To those kind, determined women who led me to Beatrix: Alison James, Anne Hunt,
Mandy Marshall, and Linda Lear; and to kind, determined girls and women everywhere, especially
Dena, Rikki, Lisa, Erin, Niomi, Julia Rose, Avigail, Lyra, Talia, Leah, Noa, Aviya, Orly, and Ellie.
— LEM

To all the creative, happy, and smart girls (of all ages) that inspire me
every day to do a better job. To Grazia Nidasio, a great artist and an inspiration,
and to Beatrix Potter for her courage and her incredible talent.
— IU

little bee books

251 Park Avenue South, New York, NY 10010
Text copyright © 2020 by Linda Elovitz Marshall
Illustrations copyright © 2020 by Ilaria Urbinati
Manufactured in China TPL 0120
First Edition
2 4 6 8 10 9 7 5 3 1

Library of Congress Cataloging-in-Publication Data
Names: Marshall, Linda Elovitz, author. | Urbinati, Ilaria, illustrator.
Title: Saving the countryside: the story of Beatrix Potter and Peter Rabbit
/ Linda Elovitz Marshall; Ilaria Urbinati. | Description: New York, New York: Little Bee Books, [2020] |
Identifiers: LCCN 2019017702 | Subjects: LCSH: Potter, Beatrix, 1866–1943—Juvenile literature. |
Authors, English—20th century—Biography—Juvenile literature. | Artists—Great Britain—Biography—
Juvenile literature. | Children's Stories—Authorship—Juvenile literature.
Classification: LCC PR6031.O72 Z6955 2020 | DDC 823/.912 [B]—dc23
LC record available at https://lccn.loc.gov/2019017702

For more information about special discounts on bulk purchases,
please contact Little Bee Books at sales@littlebeebooks.com.

ISBN 978-1-4998-0960-2
littlebeebooks.com

SAVING THE COUNTRYSIDE

THE STORY OF BEATRIX POTTER AND PETER RABBIT

words by LINDA ELOVITZ MARSHALL

pictures by ILARIA URBINATI

little bee books

On the third floor of a London town house,
a young girl sketched pictures of her pet rabbit, Benjamin Bouncer.
She also drew frogs, salamanders, turtles, and mice she had rescued from traps.

Her name was Beatrix Potter,
and she loved nature and the countryside.
But she lived in the city.

Beatrix and her younger brother, Bertram,
were cared for and taught by nannies and governesses.
They did not go to school or play with other children.

Every day, at the same time, they had lessons.
Every day, at the same time, they went on walks.

And every day, at the same time,
their mother went to visit her friends
and their father went to his social club.

Then came summer and . . .

freedom!

Beatrix and her family, and even their pets, moved to the countryside.
She and Bertram gathered eggs from chickens, fed ducklings from a spoon,
and got fresh milk from cows.

Beatrix loved the gardens with their lettuces, beans, and cabbages.
Benjamin Bouncer loved the gardens, too!

But summer,
and the freedom of the countryside,
didn't last forever.

One fall, Bertram went away to school,
which was proper for a boy of his social class.
Beatrix stayed home, as was then proper for a girl.
She was not expected to travel, attend college, or work.
But Beatrix wanted to do something important,
something that mattered.

She often helped her father with his hobby, photography.
Together, they visited artists' studios, art exhibitions, and museums.
She learned from the artists and their work.
She noticed fine details and tiny differences in facial expressions.
Inspired, Beatrix went back to sketching.

Using delicate, precise strokes,
she sketched Benjamin Bouncer.

She drew him from the front.

She drew him from the side.

She even drew him standing
and wearing fancy clothes.

Although women like her were not supposed to have careers,
Beatrix sent her sketches to publishers anyway.
She still wanted to do something important,
something that mattered.

One publisher, thinking she was a man, asked "the gentleman artist" for more pictures.
Beatrix sent more . . .
and she landed a job!
Benjamin Bouncer landed one, too.

He began appearing on holiday cards
and Beatrix Potter began earning money.

Beatrix also spent time studying and drawing nature.
Using Bertram's microscope, she examined mushrooms.
She wrote a paper about her discoveries and submitted it
to a scientific journal published by the Linnean Society.

But the scientists in charge, who were all men,
would not seriously consider her work.

Sad and disappointed,
Beatrix returned to drawing bunnies.

One day, Beatrix's young friend, Noel Moore, was feeling ill.
To cheer him up, she wrote him a story about a naughty little rabbit named Peter
who nibbled grumpy old Mr. McGregor's lettuce . . . and came very close to being caught.

Later, she called her story *The Tale of Peter Rabbit* and made it into a small book,
just the right size for little hands.

The Tale of Peter Rabbit was of no interest to most publishers.
One publisher considered it,
but he took such a long time,
and Beatrix could not keep waiting.

So, using money she'd earned from drawing Benjamin Bouncer on holiday cards,
Beatrix had 250 copies of *The Tale of Peter Rabbit* printed.

She put the books up for sale.
Every copy sold!

She ordered more copies.
They sold, too!

The Tale of Peter Rabbit was such a success
that, at last, the publisher made her an offer.
Beatrix Potter struck a deal!

Beatrix made sure that her beautiful little books
would not cost too much.
She wanted everyone to be able to buy them.

Beatrix kept writing stories:
The Tailor of Gloucester, The Tale of the Flopsy Bunnies, The Tale of Benjamin Bunny, and others. In all, she wrote twenty-three little books!

She illustrated her stories with pictures of
cottages and gardens, faraway hills,
country villages, farms, lakes,
forests, and ancient stone bridges . . .
all the places she loved.

She also designed toys, games, and tea sets,
and she put pictures of Peter Rabbit on them.
She turned Peter Rabbit into a "character."

Beatrix wanted everyone, everywhere,
to know that Peter Rabbit was her idea.
To protect her creations, she copyrighted her work.

Beatrix Potter, a woman who was not supposed to have a career,
had created something important.
She had created something that mattered.
And she became an excellent businesswoman.

Soon, people all over the world knew about Peter Rabbit,
and they knew about Beatrix Potter, too.

But Beatrix missed country life.
So, even though unmarried women were not supposed to buy property,
Beatrix bought herself a farm!

She bought cows and pigs, too.
And Herdwick sheep, a breed unique to the area.

A few years later, Beatrix bought a second farm,
and she married a man who also enjoyed country life.

But Beatrix was growing older.
She was changing.
Her fingers were getting stiff,
and her eyesight was weakening.
She could no longer draw and paint
in the delicate, precise way she always had.

The countryside, too, was changing.
Roads were widened and paved.
Forests were sold. Trees were chopped down.
Houses were built where there had once been farm fields.

Little by little, the landscape that Beatrix loved—
the farms, gardens, and cottages she painted—
was disappearing.

The country was becoming more like the city.

So Beatrix turned her attention
to protecting the natural world—
the world that she, and Peter Rabbit, loved.

She bought another farm . . .

and another . . .
and then another.

She bought cottages and gardens, farms and forests.
To save the countryside that inspired her books,
Beatrix Potter bought as much land as she could.

She took care of animals and people, too.
When sheep took ill and farmers could not afford veterinary care,
Beatrix paid the veterinarian bills
and helped save the lives of many sheep.

When flu spread through the countryside
and rural families lacked medical care,
Beatrix helped arrange for a trained nurse to live in the area
and provided her with a cottage and a car.

In the end, Beatrix donated more than four thousand acres
and fifteen farms to an organization called the National Trust.
She made sure the land would be cared for, protected, and cherished. Forever.

So today, the cottages and gardens, hills, farms,
lakes, and forests of the English Lake District
still look much like they did when Peter Rabbit
first hopped into Mr. McGregor's garden.

Beatrix Potter
did something important,
something that mattered.
She made millions of people,
especially children,
happy.

With the help of her storybook friend, Peter Rabbit,
Beatrix Potter rescued farms, animals, and wildlife.

Together, they helped save the countryside . . .
for all living things to enjoy.

THE END

Author's Note

In 2018, I participated in a "literary ramble," visiting England with a group of children's authors and illustrators. We traveled to places that inspired Roald Dahl, Lewis Carroll, Lucy Boston, Kenneth Grahame, J. K. Rowling, and many others.

On arrival in Near Sawrey, in the Lake District where Beatrix Potter had lived, my heart did a flip-flop! It was March, a rather dreary time of the year, yet the countryside—the hills, lakes, and farms—sang to me. How could it be that, after so many years, the area looked exactly as it did in Beatrix Potter's little books? Had time stood still? How was it possible that the area was so undeveloped, so peaceful, quiet, and charming? It was a mystery to me.

Our group stayed in Tom Kitten's house (now the delightful Buckle Yeat Guest House), and visited Hill Top, Beatrix's first property in the area, as well as the Beatrix Potter Gallery, and Castle Cottage, the second of Beatrix Potter's purchases in the Lake District. At Castle Cottage, which is cared for by the National Trust, we were treated to tea and, thanks to the caretaker/historian-in-residence, Mandy Marshall, to an introduction to the life and works of Beatrix Potter.

The mystery was solved! The Lake District looked undeveloped and peaceful because of Beatrix Potter. She helped save the area from trains running through it, from farms being split into housing developments, and from the myriad intrusions of the developments of city life. She kept the country, the country. With money she earned from Peter Rabbit and her twenty-two other little books and their "sideshows," she bought more than four thousand acres of land and donated it all to the National Trust, the United Kingdom organization that preserves places of historical or natural interest. What a woman!

Beatrix also bred and helped sustain a breed of sheep (called Herdwick) that was rapidly heading toward extinction. She helped farm wives set up tea shops to supplement their family income, provided medical care for rural families, and supplied veterinary support for farmers whose budgets were stretched to the limit.

This was the legacy through which Beatrix Potter "spoke" to me. Long ago, I too raised sheep. My sheep are gone now, as are my chickens and rabbits. Even my farm dogs are gone. And, as the noises of the city and civilization encroach on my farm, much of the peace and quiet is gone, too.

But thanks to Beatrix Potter, *The Tale of Peter Rabbit*, and the many people who help preserve open spaces, there are still quiet country places where children, and rabbits, can run through the fields freely and nibble a carrot. Or two.

SOURCES

Dennison, Matthew. *Over the Hills and Far Away: The Life of Beatrix Potter*. New York: Pegasus Books, 2017.

Fabiny, Sarah and Mike Lacey. *Who Was Beatrix Potter?* New York: Grosset & Dunlap, 2015.

Hallinan, Camilla. *The Ultimate Peter Rabbit*. New York: DK Children, 2016.

Lane, Margaret. *The Tale of Beatrix Potter*. New York: Frederick Warne & Co., 2014.

Lear, Linda. *Beatrix Potter: A Life in Nature*. New York: St. Martin's Griffin, 2016.

Potter, Beatrix and Leslie Linder. *The Journal of Beatrix Potter* (abridged). With an introduction by Glen Cavaliero. New York: Frederick Warne & Co., 1986; online ed., 2011.

Schonfeld, Sara (adaptor). *The Tale of Beatrix Potter*. New York: Penguin Young Readers, 2016.

Wallner, Alexandra. *Beatrix Potter*. New York: Holiday House, 1995.

And, of course, thanks to the places that inspired this work: Hill Top and Castle Cottage in Near Sawrey; and the very informative exhibition *The Right Sort of Woman* at the Beatrix Potter Gallery in Hawkshead, United Kingdom.

With special thanks and appreciation to Linda Lear, historian, Beatrix Potter expert, and the author of one of the above-mentioned works, for welcoming me and guiding me on this journey into the fabulous life of Beatrix Potter.